THE SALVATION ARM

A PICTORIAL RECORD

CHARLOTTE HORRIDGE

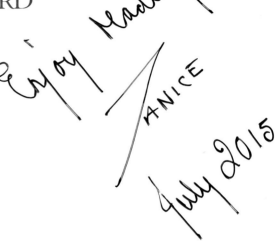

Enjoy Mark
Janice
July 2015

AMMONITE BOOKS
GODALMING

First published 1989
©Charlotte Horridge 1989

Ammonite Books
58 Coopers Rise
Godalming
Surrey GU7 2NJ

Typeset by Coorlea Publishing, Taverham Hall, Norwich.
Printed by Haynes Cannon, Park Farm Estate, Wellingborough.

ISBN 1 869866 04 5

ACKNOWLEDGEMENTS

I would like to thank the following for photographs, information and help so freely given: John and Sue Janaway, Mike Petty (Head of the Cambridgeshire Collection at Cambridge Central Library), Mr D.Read, Mr P.Read, Mrs Lt.Col.Stevens-Munn and members of my family. I must also mention the late Lt.Col.F.K.Stevens-Munn of Ilfracombe, a Salvation Army Officer for many years, whose knowledge proved invaluable.

INTRODUCTION

The work of the Salvation Army began in a tent on a disused East London Quaker burial ground in July 1865. 124 years later, the Army's evangelistic campaigns have reached global proportions. Its officers, in ensuring that people are 'saved to be saved', have visited North and South America, Africa, India, Russia, Australasia and virtually every other conceivable part of the world. At present the Army is at work in over 80 countries.

The founder of this movement was born at 12, Notintone Place, Sneinton, Nottingham, on 10th April 1829. William Booth was the third of five children, although the eldest, Henry, had died in 1828. Due to some unsuccessful business endeavours, William's father, Samuel, was forced into extreme circumstances and the family existed barely above the poverty line. Various events in William's formative years served to emphasize the poverty in his life and in the lives of those around him. It was the late 1830s and early 1840s, the 'hungry forties', which witnessed the most acute unemployment amongst the working classes. William was luckier than many children in the period before compulsory schooling. His parents understood the value of education and he was fortunate to remain at school until the age of 13.

In 1842 William was apprenticed in the ever thriving business of pawnbroking. Each day he witnessed pathetic scenes as hundreds pawned their few possessions, such as Sunday clothes, in order to have food to eat.

The Booth family themselves were edging closer to poverty for shortly after the young William left school, his father died. His mother, Mary, and the four children were forced to move to a very small house and shop premises, where she eked out a precarious living selling needles, cottons, threads and wools. William's weekly wage of six shillings was the family's only steady income. It is therefore not surprising that, during the early 1840s, William became influenced by the speeches and notions of the Chartists, which found fertile ground among the unemployed of Nottingham.

This dalliance with the Chartists was only brief. Although he was nominally a member of the Church of England, William regularly attended Wesleyan Chapel. Initially the services made little impression, but in 1844, shortly before his fifteenth birthday, William became aware of God and was converted.

As a zealous religious worker, William was soon spending all his spare time preaching in the streets and villages, or attending the Wesleyan Chapel in Nottingham. He was greatly influenced by the American revivalist, the Rev. James Caughey, who conducted meetings at Nottingham in 1846. In the same year William became an official lay preacher. He was much concerned for the poverty all around him and, on one occasion, he took several of the poorest working class into the main body of the chapel for the service. This outraged many of the regular congregation and William was told firmly that, in future, he must bring such people in by the back door and sit them on the benches especially set aside for them.

At the end of his six-year apprenticeship as a pawnbroker William failed to find a job. Therefore, in the Autumn of 1849 he made his way to London, where the only employment he was offered was in a pawnbrokers. His faith was undaunted and his preaching qualities brought him recognition and help from Mr. E.H.Rabbits, a member of the Methodist Reform Movement. In 1852, William became a full time preacher for the Reformers but three months later, on his 23rd birthday, he terminated this engagement. Until the November of 1852 he was again living in poverty whilst contemplating a future as a Congregationalist minister. However, he took charge of a Methodist Reform Circuit at Spalding, Lincolnshire, where he remained for 18 months.

William had already met the major influence of his life shortly before his 23rd birthday. At a tea party organised by Mr. Rabbits in early 1852, he was introduced to Catherine Mumford. Born at Ashbourne, Derbyshire, Catherine was two months older than William. She was mostly home educated and not of particularly strong health, but she had very fixed ideas about female equality, temperance, foreign missionary work, the poor and religion in general. It was Catherine who supported William's move to the Reformers in April 1852, his thoughts on Congregationalism, his return to the Reformers and his eventual mainstay of the Methodist New Connexion in 1854.

William and Catherine were married on 16th June 1855 and immediately began a nationwide revivalist campaign together. In November 1857 they reluctantly accepted confinement to another circuit, this time Brighouse in Yorkshire. During the Booth's time there, a meeting with the Rev. Caughey convinced the unhappy couple that they should stay at least until William's ordination, which took place in 1858. In that year William and Catherine, with their two children, Bramwell and Ballington, moved to Gateshead, where they remained for three years. At Gateshead their preaching was so successful that the Bethesda Chapel became known as the 'Converting Shop'. It was here on the morning of Sunday, 8th January 1860 that Catherine first spoke publicly to the congregation. Later, when her husband was ill she took charge — a very unusual and courageous act in the male dominated Victorian era.

The Booth's resignation from the Methodist New Connexion came at the conference of 1861 with Catherine's famous public exclamation of refusal, after the voting, to accept another circuit. There then followed four years of hard evangelistic campaigning before the couple reached the East End of London and the tent mission.

The Home Mission movement had developed from the initiatives of both churches and individuals concerned about the overcrowding and deprivation of the unchurched masses in the inner cities. The tent mission at the time of Booth's arrival was known as the Christian Revival Association. William was invited to lead it. His objective was to convert those unchurched masses and then send them out to churches and chapels. He was very successful with the former, but the problems started when his converts would not leave and if they did, they were often not welcome elsewhere. William also began to appreciate that, with the rapid growth of the mission, he needed co-workers. The mission became known as the East London Christian Mission. It continued to increase in numbers and spread geographically, and thus the name was changed to the Christian Mission.

When the tent had to be abandoned, a dancing 'saloon' was hired for Sundays. After spending some hours clearing and cleaning the saloon, the typical pattern of the day for the Booths included three indoor meetings, three processions and three or four open air meetings. William mainly concentrated on the east of the city whilst Catherine went elsewhere, including the West End. She led the way to opening other mission stations. One station used by the Booths was the once infamous Effingham Theatre and another, the equally iniquitous Eastern Star. In October 1868 the Mission began the publication of its own magazine, *The East London Evangelist*. In 1870 an annual conference was called, but within a few years the organisation had become too large to be effectively represented in this way and the idea was dropped.

Britain in the 1870s was the pivot of a rapidly expanding empire over which many of its inhabitants claimed 'the sun never set'. Jingoism and militarism were rife. Therefore, it seemed only natural that the General Superintendent of the Mission should allow his Mission officers to call him 'General', to adopt military titles for themselves and to talk in fighting terms. After all, they were engaged in the fight against sin. Thus, probably in early May 1878, William Booth decided that the Christian Mission was not a volunteer army but a full-time army seeking the salvation of the world — The Salvation Army. Once the name was adopted, British Army terminology came into use. Stations became 'corps', missioners became 'officers', and flags, uniforms and bands soon followed. The adoption of the British Army's methods of organisation and discipline proved very effective.

The Salvation Army quickly established itself in strength throughout the United Kingdom. In 1880 it expanded to the United States of America under George Scott Railton. France, Switzerland, India and a host of other countries were similarly invaded. Furious opposition was often encountered, mainly from the drink trade who used the police, magistrates and mob rule in an attempt to expel the Army from some towns. Such tactics served only to highlight the work of the movement.

William and Catherine established the firm base for an evangelical movement of worldwide vision. Despite the death of the 'Army Mother' from cancer on 4th October 1890, William carried on the fight for a further 22 years. Both the Booths were prodigious writers and William's social scheme, worked out in his *In Darkest England and the Way Out*, was of profound significance in the development of the welfare state. Many new ideas were brought together in this book. Thus, social work and evangelism, a formula used successfully by the Booths for many years, became a widely accepted means of reaching the masses.

The entire Booth family worked for the conversion of mankind. William, Catherine and their eight children, plus the officers and soldiers were totally dedicated to this task. There were indeed 'deserters' for various reasons, but the spirit of William Booth remains to prove the words of his final speech:
'While women weep, as they do now, I'll fight; while little children go hungry, as they do now, I'll fight; while men go to prison, in and out, as they do now, I'll fight; while there is a drunkard left, while there is a poor lost girl upon the street, while there remains one dark soul without the light of God, I'll fight — I'll fight to the very end!'

Charlotte Horridge
Cambridge
September 1989.

To my husband, Kenneth.

Yours very affectionately,
William Booth

1. A picture presented to the Rev. William Booth on 26th November 1856 by his Methodist New Connexion friends in Sheffield 'in appreciation of his arduous, zealous and successful labours there and in other parts of the community'. William was accepted as a minister by the New Connexion's annual conference in 1854 and he worked for them until the early 1860s.

2. William Booth's birthplace, 12 Notintone Place, Sneinton, Nottingham. The house, which is owned by the Salvation Army, now contains a small but interesting museum. Neighbouring the General's first home is an Army complex, opened in 1971, consisting of an Eventide Home for fifty residents, a goodwill centre and a family rehabilitation unit.

MRS. BOOTH
(the Mother of our General).

3. William's mother, Mary, who died on 13th January 1875, aged 84, was the daughter of a well-to-do farmer, Joseph Moss, and was born at Somercotes, near Alfreton in Derbyshire.

4. William's wife, Catherine, was born on 17th January 1829 at Ashbourne in Derbyshire. She was never particularly strong in health and much of her childhood was spent in reading religious books, especially the Bible.

5. Sarah Mumford, Catherine Booth's mother, had been brought up by her widowed father and her aunt, and all three regularly attended their parish church. The Methodists purchased land for a chapel from Sarah's father and soon after she became an ardent convert.

6. This chapel was of great importance to the young William Booth. Although he had supported the Chartists in the early 1840s, he turned to religion as the way of man's salvation and became a Methodist. The American revivalist, the Rev. James Caughey, who campaigned in Nottingham, made a major impression upon William, who particularly admired him for the way he appealed to the populace. It was in this chapel that William Booth first emulated the spirit of Caughey's preaching.

7. This Nottingham cottage meeting in 1845 was one of many conducted by William Booth. His first sermon had been delivered in similar circumstances one evening in Kid Street, Nottingham, to a small group composed mainly of women. Even at 17 years of age, he was an eloquent speaker but, more importantly, he talked in terms which his audience could easily understand and identify with. He was, after all, one of the people.

8. This early photograph shows William and Catherine in typical Victorian pose. The couple became officially engaged on 5th May 1852, but did not marry for over three years because of William's uncertain future with various religious groups. They were finally married on 16th June 1855 in Stockwell New Chapel in South London. Both were 26 years of age and had already become a well suited team. They remained exceedingly happy throughout their life together.

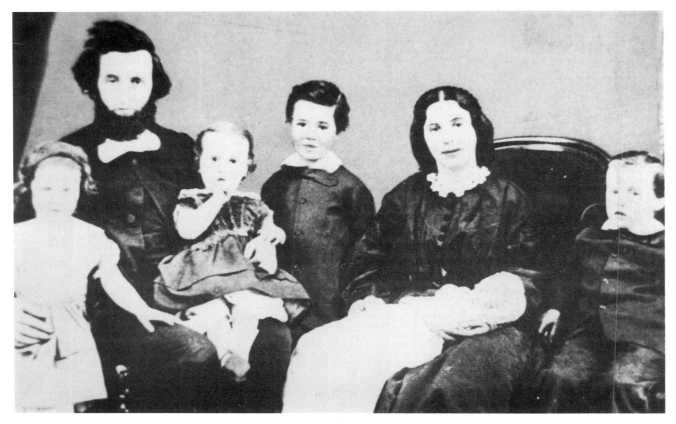

9. This family portrait shows William and Catherine with five of their children: Catherine, Emma, William Bramwell, Herbert and Ballington. It dates from about October 1862, shortly after William's resignation from the Methodist New Connexion had been accepted.

10. It was at the Annual Conference in Liverpool on 20th May 1861, that William was refused permission to become a full-time itinerant evangelist, but a compromise was suggested. At this point Catherine loudly and emphatically shouted from the gallery, 'Never!'. As a result, William reluctantly tendered his resignation.

11. William Booth preaching on the Mile End Waste on 5th July 1865, shortly before he began his work with the Tent Mission. The prominent building in the centre is 'The Vine' public house in the Mile End Road. At this time the Booth family were living at 31 Shaftesbury Road, Hammersmith.

12. William Booth preaching in the Effingham Theatre, Whitechapel Road, London − a venue which he used regularly on Sunday evenings from early 1867. William Booth had a powerful but simple formula when preaching, as he had used earlier in Nottingham − he was identifiable as one of the working class and he spoke to the people in easily understandable terms. The number of meetings at this theatre increased after it had been rebuilt and renamed the East London Theatre.

13. The People's Mission Hall was opened on Sunday, 10th April 1870. The premises cost, including alterations, well over £3,000 and the annual ground rent amounted to £135. The Hall, at 272 Whitechapel Road, also served as Booth's headquarters. Here, innumerable people were converted and many important events in the history of the Salvation Army took place, including the 1878 War Congress. The Hall later became part of the 'city colony'.

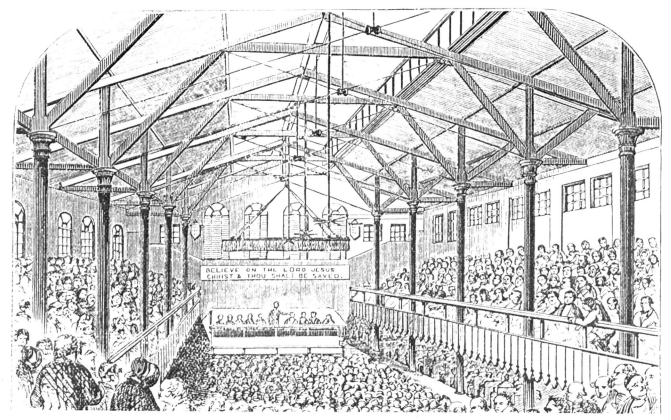

BELIEVE ON THE LORD JESUS
CHRIST & THOU SHALT BE SAVED.

14. This engraving of the interior of the People's Mission Hall well illustrates the popularity of the meetings held there. For the first time in its history the Christian Mission could hold a variety of meetings without the worry of running over time. The Mission could dispense cheap but wholesome food and also run a number of other missionary activities.

15. This portrait shows General William Booth in Salvation Army uniform. It was Capt. Elijah Cadman who, at the 1878 War Congress, made the first public demand for a uniform, albeit initially for officers only. Immediately after the Congress Salvationists began to identify themselves by wearing badges attached to hats or sleeves. In 1880, an attempt was made in various issues of *The War Cry* to regularise the increasing variety of military uniforms worn by officers and soldiers. The price of a male officer's uniform was 21/6 (£1.07p) or 36/6 (£1.82p), depending on the quality of the material, whilst a soldier's uniform was 6d (2.5p) cheaper in both cases.

16. Catherine Booth, the 'Army Mother', was a striking figure in full uniform. The 19th century bonnet made its first appearance in any numbers when worn by 25 cadets on 16th June 1880, the silver wedding anniversary of General and Mrs Booth. The bonnet was a large straw affair, trimmed with black silk and wide black ribbons. In this portrait Catherine gives prominence to her much valued wedding ring. Shortly before her death, on 4th October 1890, she returned the ring to William who in turn, upon his own death-bed, sent it to their daughter, Evangeline.

17. Florence Eleanor Soper was just 19 when she accompanied General Booth's eldest daughter, Catherine, to France in 1881 to commence the Army's work there. On 12th October 1882, Florence married Bramwell Booth at the new Clapton Congress Hall, where the 6,000 people attending the service were charged 1/- (5p) admission. Here they heard General Booth proclaim the Chief-of-Staff, Bramwell, as the next General if he should die in office.

18. Bramwell Booth is seen here playing with three of his children at their house, 'The Homestead', at Hadley Wood. Florence and Bramwell had seven children: Catherine, Mary, Miriam, Bernard, Olive, Dora and Wycliffe. It was an extremely happy family, who were close not only to their paternal grandfather, the General, but also to their maternal grandfather, Dr. Soper of Plymouth.

SALVATION ARMY CONGRESS HALL LOWER CLAPTON.

19. The Clapton Congress Hall in Linscott Road had previously been the London Orphan Asylum. It was bought in November 1881 for conversion into a place of worship and for use as a training barracks. The total cost was £23,000 and it was opened by General Booth on Saturday, 13th May 1882. His appeal for donations at the opening meeting, to make up the shortfall of £8,000, was met in less than two weeks.

20. The large hall at Clapton was often packed solid, as this 1882 view of the interior shows. An orchestra is situated just below the platform, which is surrounded by handkerchief waving members of the congregation. Within the confines of the premises, cadets were drilled and taught, being roused by bugle and whistle at 6 a.m. each morning. By the end of 1882, 440 cadets had been trained at Clapton.

21. A number of High Wycombe soldiers are seen here outside their barracks in 1882. Their uniforms show some attempt at standardisation and most soldiers appear to be wearing a badge of some sort denoting the Salvation Army. 1882 was a year of rapid growth for the Army, often in the face of violent opposition. At least 669 soldiers were 'brutally assaulted' and 56 buildings used by the Army attacked during that year.

22. The Army suffered violent opposition in a number of southern towns. The mobs sometimes organised themselves into 'skeleton armies', which often marched behind a banner depicting a skeleton and whose favourite activity was the disruption of open air meetings. Here the opposition at Worthing is seen stoning the barracks in 1884. The mob also stoned the police station and caused serious damage to other property. Only the arrival of troops restored order.

23. The stoning of barracks by mobs only reinforced the determination of soldiers to maintain their witness. Here is the Brighton Congress Hall following one such attack in 1884. The hall could seat 3,500 and cost over £7,000 to build, the entire sum being contributed by a local couple. The Army hired, built or commenced a total of 85 buildings during 1884.

24. The Army's official arrival in Guildford took place on Sunday, 19th December 1881, when two 'Hallelujah Lasses' attracted several hundred people to their meeting place. Although the Army was well supported by many of the town's leading citizens, it also faced violent opposition in this Surrey market town. Here, one of the original officers, Captain Knight, is shown being kicked and beaten in the street.

25. Fortunately, in the majority of communities in Britain the Army was quickly accepted and usually welcomed. Here we see a crowded open air meeting with the ever popular big bass drum doubling as a receptacle for contributions. The drum also frequently served as a penitent-form, where people became converted. At the end of each meeting it returned to its original functions of attracting attention and of beating out the rhythm of the march.

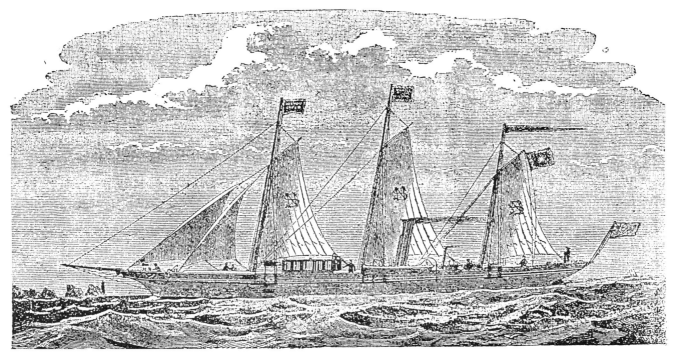

26. The steam yacht *Iole* was given to the General by John Cory of Cardiff in June 1885. She was the first vessel of the Salvation Navy and gave much encouragement to trawler captains to fly the Army flag. The *Iole* sank, fortunately without loss of life, after hitting a sandbank whilst entering the Humber on 19th June 1886.

27. Evangeline Cory Booth, William and Catherine's fourth daughter, was born on Christmas Day 1865. At a very young age she quickly became a prominent figure in Army work. 'Eva' developed an 'action woman' image both in promoting the Army's work and in her private life, becoming an accomplished horsewoman, swimmer and diver. Although she never married, a number of suitors presented themselves – most notably Major (later Commissioner) McKie and the Russian, Prince Galitzin. Eva became the fourth General of the Salvation Army, holding that office from 1934 to 1939.

28. This rare postcard shows General Booth happily surrounded by twelve of his numerous grandchildren. Although the General was often severe with his eight offspring and their children, he nevertheless loved them all.

29. Florence Booth was born in London on 18th June 1887. She was the third of Bramwell Booth's seven children and was always known by her second name of Miriam. In May 1910 she became a cadet at the International Training Garrison. Although Miriam suffered ill health throughout much of her time as an officer, she continued to write and work zealously. When she died, her aunt, Commander Evangeline Booth wrote of her: 'Her ministry was brief, but it was marvellously rich and far-reaching. Her physical sufferings were great, but her spirit rose above them in self-forgetting zeal for others'.

30. The Carlisle Citadel Band was one of many large northern Salvation Army bands of the Edwardian period. The Army's love of music greatly appealed to many northerners. This picture dates from 1910 when the Carlisle I Corps had been in existence for about 30 years.

31. These two pages illustrate examples of Salvation Army pin-flags dating from the First World War.

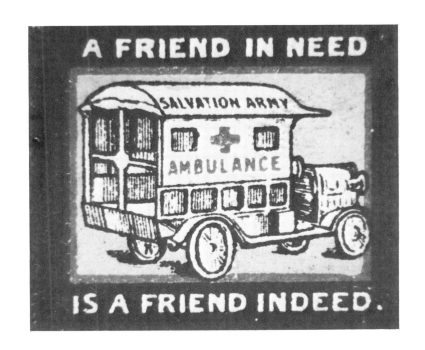

32. Street collection was an important means of raising funds to provide comforts for the troops and finance for the much needed ambulance service.

33. Another prominent Army band, the Cambridge Heath Band, are pictured here on the eve of the First World War. General Booth encouraged music in the promotion of the Gospel and to attract attention to the Army. Even before the first official Army bands were established at Salisbury and Consett, music played an important role in his services.

34. The Boscombe Band is one of many Army bands which have retained a high reputation over several generations. The white straps across the bandsmen's braided tunics carry a black leather pouch containing the sheets of music. As is usual in such pictures, the corps officers are seated in the centre of the front row.

CHALK FARM BAND — MOTOR TOUR, 1911

35. Chalk Farm Band was established in 1882 with a total of nine converts. After a struggling start, the appointment in 1894 of 17 year old Alfred W. Punchard, who was bandmaster until 1938, led to the band becoming well known in many countries for its high standard of musicianship. On 9th August 1924 they became the first London band to play on the 'wireless' and, ten years later, they played at Buckingham Palace.

36. The International Headquarters of the Salvation Army at 101, Queen Victoria Street, was established in 1881. All aspects of the Army's growing international work and some domestic activities were co-ordinated from here. This very large building was destroyed by German bombs on the night of 10/11th May 1941. The present headquarters was opened by Queen Elizabeth the Queen Mother on 13th November 1963.

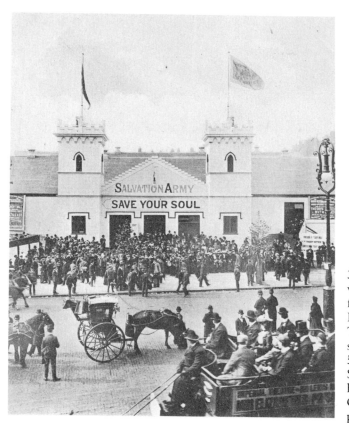

37. The Third International Congress of the Salvation Army was held from 24th June to 8th July 1904. It was based on four places in London: the International Congress Hall, The Royal Albert Hall, the Exeter Hall and the Crystal Palace. The International Congress Hall was a huge structure specifically built for the Congress, which could hold over 5,000 people. It was constructed on the site of Holywell Street, the Globe Theatre and Opera Comique, the area having been cleared for redevelopment by London County Council. The Hall was subsequently demolished and replaced by the B.B.C.'s Bush House.

38. Although the International Congress Hall had three roof spans, inside was a single almost square area. Over 6,000 delegates from 49 countries attended the Congress and each night saw large crowds attempting to jam into the already packed seating area.

39. Social relief had long been a part of William Booth's ideology, dating back to before the foundation of the Army proper. From the headquarters for women's social work in Mare Street, Hackney, the Army organised many essentially needed activities. These included the care of unmarried mothers and the rescue of prostitutes.

40. The Salvation Army Barracks at Holloway, London, prominently advertised the International Congress in 1904. Such fortress style buildings as this, complete with crenellated 'ramparts', became the typical hallmark of Army establishments of the period. Several examples of these durable buildings still survive.

41. General Booth covered thousands of miles during seven motor tours between 1904 and 1911. His second tour, in 1905, became known as 'The White Car Crusade' because of his use of a large white Darracq with red wheels. The Crusade started at Folkestone only two days after the General had returned from a tour of Australasia and the Holy Land. It ended in London following a journey of 2,250 miles through England and Scotland. Here he is seen in his motor uniform just prior to addressing the inmates of Horsham Workhouse.

42. This photograph was taken in 1906 during the General's third motor tour. Seated behind him is his eldest grandchild, Capt. Catherine Booth, then Commanding Officer at Bath. This campaign began at Inverness and ended a month later at Dartmoor Prison, where the General addressed 1,000 convicts. In addition to speaking in prisons, workhouses and theatres, he also addressed the regiments of the Black Watch and Seaforth Highlanders.

43. General Booth's fourth motor tour started in July 1907 at High Barnet and covered the eastern counties, Yorkshire, Lancashire, Wales and the South Coast of England, including Worthing. Here he temporarily abandoned his motor car for more traditional transport. He was widely welcomed in this seaside town, where twenty years earlier the Army had suffered a number of vicious attacks.

44. The day that William Booth was honoured with the Freedom of his home city was one of his happiest. It marked a considerable achievement — the rise from poverty to international fame. Only days earlier the General had received a similar accolade from the City of London.

45. General Booth attracted vast audiences wherever he preached. He is seen here addressing Salvationists at the Exeter Hall, London, on 17th November 1890. This was during one of his regular 'Two Days with God' campaigns, which he conducted throughout the United Kingdom.

46. The readily identifiable Salvation Army soon became the subject of music hall jokes, songs and sketches. In 1882, a year which saw much violent opposition to the Army, cartoons began to appear in periodicals and magazines. Such cartoons were usually directed at Booth himself and here is a typical example from that year. It was published in 7th October issue of *The Entr'acte* and raises a question which was very topical in the 1880s.

NOW, MR. BOOTH, LET US KNOW WHAT YOU ARE GOING TO DO WITH ALL THIS MONEY?

47. This cartoon also appeared in 1882, this time in *Vanity Fair*.

GENERAL BOOTH WELCOMING THE SWAZI CHIEFS AT HIS HOME

48. As a mark of the growing international work of the Army, the General often received overseas visitors. He enjoyed meeting national leaders and always spoke of the good work the Army was doing or could be doing in their respective lands.

**The Casket in which was enclosed the City of London's Freedom to General Booth
26th October, 1905.**

49. General Booth received many accolades during the last few years of his life. Although he felt himself unworthy of the honour of the Freedom of the City of London, he nevertheless accepted it as recognition that the Army 'had come to stay'. This commemorative postcard was one of a number widely circulated at the time.

50. During an international tour in 1907, the General had the rare honour of an audience with the Emperor of Japan. In June, upon his return, he was awarded the honorary degree of Doctor of Civil Law at the University of Oxford. Lord Curzon, the Chancellor of the University, said that it was given so that his university could ' ... have the privilege of setting its seal upon the noble work that you have done ... a work excelled in range and beneficence by that of no living man'.

51. Elijah Cadman, 'The Converted Chimney Sweep', who had been cleaning chimneys since before the age of six, was born in Coventry in 1843. He was converted to Methodism and avidly 'taught' the junior Sunday School class but, being illiterate, it was not easy to teach the alphabet. In the event, he relied upon the correct answers from the majority, as the means of learning for both himself and the rest of the class . He became an evangelist and, joining the Christian Mission, he took charge of Hackney Station on 5th August 1876. Elijah soon declared himself 'Captain' in the war against sin, a battle in which he fought tirelessly until his death on 12th December 1927.

52. John Lawley was born at Foulden in Norfolk on 31st December 1859. The family moved to Bradford where, at the age of seventeen, John was converted at the Christian Mission by James Dowdle, 'The Saved Guard'. He soon launched himself into full time service and became the Mission's fortieth evangelist, assuming his first command with the opening of Spennymoor Christian Mission station which commenced operations on Sunday, 28th April 1878. He travelled widely as an officer and, from 1890, was a constant companion and aide to General Booth, both at home and abroad. John Lawley died, aged 62, at Watford.

53. In 1890, General Booth published his *In Darkest England and the Way Out*, in which he outlined his solutions to the problems of the 'submerged tenth', those poorest people who were below the status of a cab-horse, which at least had food, shelter and work. His proposals included the establishment of a city colony, a farm colony and an overseas colony. This is the headquarters of the city colony at 20 and 22 Whitechapel Road, London. Before the renumbering of the road, No.22 had been No.272, the People's Mission Hall.

54. In early 1891, 800 acres of land in Essex were purchased, not far from Southend, for the establishment of a farm colony. Later, the Army bought a further 2,400 acres and here many poor men and boys were taught the many aspects of farming. This view shows some of their dormitories at the Hadleigh Farm Colony, as it was called.

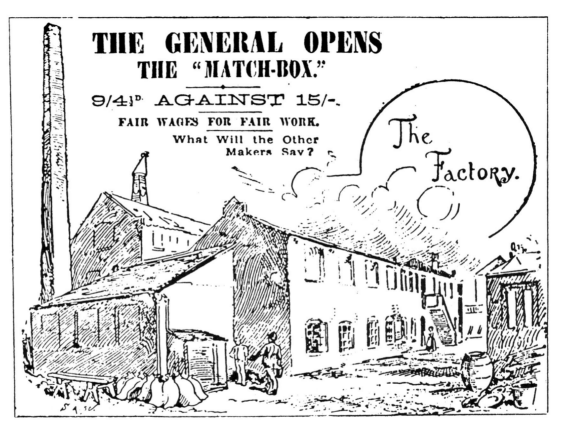

55. During the 1880s General Booth became increasingly antagonistic towards the social evils of the time. This included the sweating system and, in particular, its application to match girls. Booth set out to prove that the wages, hours and conditions could be improved and safety matches still made cheaply and successfully. He purchased a large building in Lamprell Street, London, and had it converted into a match factory. It opened in April 1891 and here 'Lights in Darkest England' brand matches were manufactured.

56. The Army's increasing awareness of social needs was crystallised in William Booth's writings. As a result, the Army established a seemingly endless variety of small factories providing employment in a good working environment, with respectable levels of pay and with the opportunity of retraining where necessary. This 1907 photograph is entitled 'Friendless girls at work in a Salvation Army knitting factory'.

57. The name of the Salvation Army is synonymous with the giving of aid, and nowhere is this more apparent than in the still continuing nightly soup kitchens. Here the police are on hand to ensure orderly waiting, whilst hundreds queue for their life-supporting bowl of hot soup.

58. This is the interior of one of the Army's shelters for men. Here, a man could have a foot-bath or a full bath whilst his clothes were washed and dried in rapid time. Food and drink were available as well as spiritual comfort.

S.A. SERVING SOUP MIDNIGHT NOV. 8. 1909
THAMES EMBANKMENT

59. At midnight on 8th November 1909, about a hundred men were photographed on the Thames Embankment, London, as they queued to receive their ration of soup. Note that not all seem properly clothed against the cold of the winter months.

60. The rescue of alcoholics has always been an important part of the Army's work. Notorious drunkards saved included Mrs Cunningham, alias Nancy Dickybird. She was perhaps Manchester's most infamous female alcoholic and she served no less than 173 terms of imprisonment. Another was Rosie Bannister, a well known Burnley alcoholic, who enlisted in the Army following her 75th appearance before the local magistrates. After her conversion she settled into respectable married life with a local mill manager.

Rosie Bannister.

61. In 1891, to augment those shelters already established in London, further shelters were opened at Blackfriars, Bethnal Green, Clare Market, Lisson Grove and Royal Mint Street. This Edwardian photograph shows the Blackfriars Shelter where many hundreds of men crowded each night, although in 1895 magistrates had limited the capacity of the building to 550.

AT "THE NEST"

62. By July 1901 'The Nest' had been established as a place of refuge for mothers with young children. However, it was not long before it began functioning solely as a girls home. In 1910, 62 girls aged between four and sixteen, many of whom had suffered neglect, abuse or abandonment, were being given shelter there. The girls followed the lead of Florence and Bramwell Booth in being vegetarians and were educated 'under the direction of a certified governess'.

Loving Birthday Greetings!

Oh, the days fly fast! you are two at
  last,
Little Sunbeam lad with your smile
  so glad,
And our hopes are high for your
  "bye-and-bye,"
So we greet this day in a gladsome
  way.

63. A series of Salvation Army postcards was produced prior
to the First World War to celebrate the birthdays of children
attached to the Corps. This particular card was sent from
Ebbw Vale on 28th February 1914.

Loving Birthday Greetings!

Let us say once more to our boy of
  four
We are glad for you as the years we
  view
As their hours have flown you have
  learned and grown,
So may all your days to our God
  bring praise.

64. Two years later, the same little boy received this card. Although the format remained the same, the verse and picture had changed.

As Actress.   FLORENCE WORTH, Converted Actress.   As Salvationist.

65. This is a typical example of an Army 'before and after' postcard, popular around the turn of the century. Any figure likely to be nationally known was a highly favoured subject for the propaganda war against sin.

66. A postcard of the founder, William Booth, in the last years of his life. When the General died the Editor of *Punch*, Sir Owen Seaman, paid tribute in verse, including these lines:-

Scorned or acclaimed, he kept his
harness bright,
Still through the darkest hour,
untaught to yield,
And at the last, his face toward
the light,
Fell on the victor's field.

67. Several thousands of Salvationists and civilians attended the Founder's funeral at Abney Park Cemetery in Stoke Newington, London, on 29th August 1912. His death, as with all Salvationists, was seen as a 'Promotion to Glory' and, as with any such promotion, was 'celebrated' by the wearing of white armbands and sashes. His passing was lamented by royalty, churchmen and laymen alike all over the world. King George V sent a wreath, as did Kaiser Wilhelm of Germany and the American Ambassador on behalf of President Taft.

GENERAL
and
MRS. BOOTH

Commissioner
CARLETON

Commissioner
HIGGINS

THE CHIEF
of THE STAFF

Commissioner
McALONAN

Commissioner
COX

68. William Bramwell Booth, who was usually known by his second name, succeeded his father as the Army's second General. Bramwell is pictured here with his most senior advisers.

ADJUTANT & MRS. TED FLEMING.

69. This 1911 postcard from the commanding officers of one of the Manchester corps carries a Christmas greeting from them on the reverse. Note the less than immaculate uniforms of these hard-working 'front line' officers.

70. By the Edwardian period, violent opposition to the Army had been entirely replaced by good natured humour. Here the band is the butt of the joke. This postcard was bought and posted in Nottingham in June 1903.

71. The International Staff Songsters were formed in 1897, under the leadership of Brig. Herbert J.Jackson. Officers and employees of International Headquarters were eligible to join. The Songsters travelled extensively throughout Great Britain.

72. Some twenty years before the First World War, the Army formed a 'Naval and Military League', aimed at the all round welfare of servicemen. Alongside these developments, an ambulance fleet was established in 1914. It was not long before the Salvationists staffing the ambulances formed a band, which played in hospitals, convalescent homes and indeed anywhere where troops could be ministered to.

73. This is one of a popular series of postcards, each decorated with an Army flag and other emblems such as the Army crest, and including a text or song.

74. In this postcard from the Salvation Army Flag Series, the cornet and tambourine symbolise the musical witness of the Army. The movement's flag is intertwined with the Union Jack to emphasize the Army's origins. The song is the original version of Gustavus Grozinsky's well loved acclamation of loyalty to the flag and thus to Christianity.

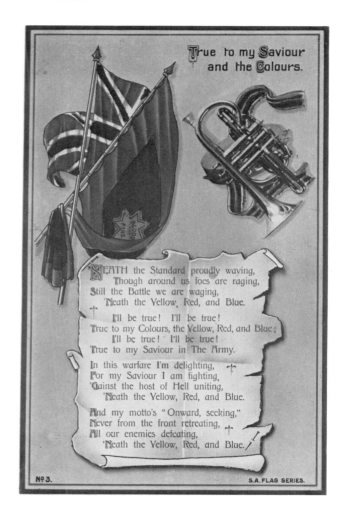

True to my Saviour and the Colours.

NEATH the Standard proudly waving,
  Though around us foes are raging,
Still the Battle we are waging,
  'Neath the Yellow, Red, and Blue.

  I'll be true! I'll be true!
True to my Colours, the Yellow, Red, and Blue;
  I'll be true! I'll be true!
True to my Saviour in The Army.

In this warfare I'm delighting,
For my Saviour I am fighting,
'Gainst the host of Hell uniting,
  'Neath the Yellow, Red, and Blue.

And my motto's "Onward, seeking,"
Never from the front retreating,
All our enemies defeating,
  'Neath the Yellow, Red, and Blue.

No 3.

S.A. FLAG SERIES.

E.H. MILLS.

75. Bramwell Booth was the Army's second General from the death of his father in 1912 until 13th February 1929. Bramwell was 'Promoted to Glory' on 16th June of the same year. He had continued to build on his father's work and had seen an increase in membership and in the numbers of countries 'invaded'. These included Latvia and Estonia in Eastern Europe, Kenya in Africa, and Brazil in South America.

76. The Bramwell Booths were a well suited couple. Bramwell was happy to capture the young Florence Soper's heart, and she delighted to put her all into the Army's work. Florence served wholeheartedly at home and abroad, and included in her special ministry work among prostitutes. She loved home life and, in 1907, inaugurated the Home League, a women's fellowship which met weekly. One of her greatest delights was to work among children and she zealously promoted all the Army's young people's movements.

77. This 1917 photograph shows the Bethnal Green 'Self Denial' collectors. 'Self Denial' originated in 1886 during a meeting at the Exeter Hall in London, when Maj. John Carleton promised to do without puddings for a year, thus saving, he calculated, fifty shillings (£2.50p). The General's alternative proposal was that all should deny themselves some food for a week. The first 'Self Denial Week' raised £4,820 and the scheme continues successfully to this day.

78. On Wednesday, 17th November 1915, Florence Booth inaugurated the Life-Saving Guards. The Army already had the Life-Saving Scouts (1913) and, a few years later, were to come the Chum Brigade (1919) and the Sunbeams (1921) — now incorporated in the Scouts, Guides, Cubs and Brownies respectively. The Guards motto was 'To Save and To Serve'. This postcard shows the highly efficient Newbiggin-by-Sea Guard troop in 1926.

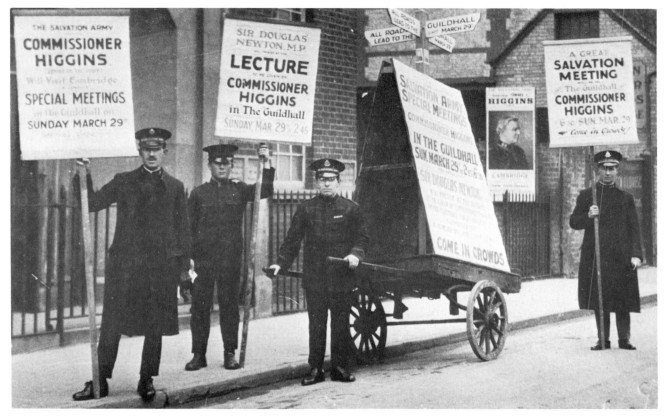

79. Cambridge Salvationists photographed outside their Citadel in Tenison Road during the few days preceding a visit by Commissioner Higgins. The Commissioner led meetings in the Cambridge Guildhall on 29th March 1925.

80. The Cambridge Citadel Salvation Army Band was photographed in 1930 whilst visiting Kings College Chapel for a Buffaloes' Service. They are marching past the Chapel led by Bandmaster C.B.Mott.

ILFRACOMBE SELF DENIAL EFFORT 1925.,
THE LOCAL OFFICERS,
(CAPT. L. MONTGOMERY.)   (LIEUT. BIRCHENOUGH.)

81. 'Self Denial' door to door collecting in the hilly North Devon countryside was a very different matter from the same work in densely populated towns and cities. Nevertheless, the officers and soldiers gladly went out, not merely to collect money but also to spread the gospel. Lt. Birchenough's married name was Church and her son is now a Divisional Commander in the United States of America.

82. From April 1928, Bramwell Booth's health began to cause grave concern. In order to ensure the continued efficient running of the Army, and the nomination of a non-hereditary successor, a High Council met at Sunbury Court on 8th January 1929. Three days later a deputation called on him at his Southwold home to suggest to him that he should retire on the grounds of ill-health. To the present day the High Council is still called each time to elect a new General.

83. These officer cadets found time off from their studies to play in the International Training Garrison Band of 1924–1925. The band formed an integral part of garrison life, accompanying fellow cadets on marches and during meetings. Cadets with any musical talent were encouraged to participate in music making, for the Army has always understood the effectiveness of music in spreading the message of Salvation.

84. The Salvationist Publishing & Supplies Ltd. or 'Trade' as it is generally referred to, was one of several sections which had a flourishing band or songster brigade during the inter-war years. Others were the Men's Social Headquarters Band, the International Staff Band, the Assurance Singers, and the Salvation Singers. The S.P. & S. Band was photographed in 1929 with Commissioner Wilson and bandmaster, Capt. Eric Ball.

85. Deptford Salvation Army Band are seen here outside their Citadel in August 1927. The rope drum, which takes pride of place in the centre, was usually one of the first instruments acquired by a band. The drum was always considered vital to any open air meeting, not only for keeping the band in step, but also as a central focus during the proceedings.

THE MUSICAL TROOPERS, 1933.

86. The Musical Troopers toured the country in 1933. Under their leader, Lt.Col. Handel Boot, and their bandmaster, Edward Saywell, the 37 strong group successfully proclaimed the gospel both indoors and out. The deputy bandmaster was Bernard Adams, later bandmaster of the International Staff Band.

87. A carefully posed photograph of one of the leading Army bands of the 1930s, with the festival tunics making for a very smart appearance. This is the Wood Green Band of London, photographed in 1937, with Bandmaster George W.Reed.

88. Staines bandsmen ready to go out and proclaim the gospel through music and song.

89. Edwardian postcard humour spared no aspect of British life, the Salvation Army included. The joke is as old as the Army and is still occasionally heard today.

SALVATION LASS: "Are you saved?"
YOUNG MAN: "No, I am a reporter!"

90. A more subtle dig at both the Army and the press.

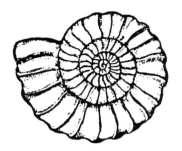

For full details of our publications please write to:

Ammonite Books
58 Coopers Rise
Godalming
Surrey GU7 2NJ